Rescuing Animals

Contents **Page**

written by John Lockyer

Animals can get sick or hurt. They can get lost, too. Rescuing animals is a job for helpers with fantastic skills.

They help our pets, farm animals, and free animals, too. The animals, can be small like a mouse or big like an elephant.

animal rescue workers

vet

Vets check out animals that are ill. They can fix cuts and bones. They make our pets feel better.

In big parks, there are helpers who look out for free animals. They check that the animals are well and not hurt.

If your pet is sick and lost, you could find it at a rescue hub. There can be lots of big and small animals at a hub.

animal rescue hub

The animals get food and water. If they are sick, they can get drugs to help them.

You can find very big animals at a rescue hub, too. They will be in a barn or a paddock.

Helpers do lots of jobs at the rescue hub. They give out food and water. They keep the animals' pens very clean.

Helpers pat the animals. They play with them, too. The big animals get to run so they keep fit.

The hub is not a home for the animals. The helpers want to find a good home for them.

new owners

A pet from a rescue hub needs a fun and happy home. They want to be well fed and have a clean place to relax and sleep.

Free animals that get sick can go to a zoo. When the animal is better it will go back to its home.

Whales can get stuck on the sand. Helpers come to help them, but they need the tide to come back in.

Helpers keep the whales wet.
They put sunblock on their skin.
Then they help them out to sea.

Rescuing animals is good. It makes the animal feel better and it makes us feel better, too.